Southbridge: My Triggering Town

Bill Tremblay

Lost Valley Press
Hardwick, MA

OTHER BOOKS BY BILL TREMBLAY

Crying in the Cheap Seats (UMass Press, 1971)

The Anarchist Heart (New Rivers Press, 1977)

Home Front (Lynx House Press, 1978)

Second Sun: New & Selected Poems (L'Epervier Press, 1985)

Duhamel: Ideas of Order in Little Canada (BOA Editions, Ltd., 1986)

The June Rise: The Apocryphal Letters of Antoine Janis [novel]
(Utah State University Press, 1994)

Rainstorm Over the Alphabet (Lynx House Press, 2001)

Shooting Script: DOOR OF FIRE (Eastern Washington University Press, 2003)

Magician's Hat, Poems on the Life and Art of David Alfaro Siqueiros
(Lynx House Press, 2013)

Walks Along the Ditch: Poems (Lynx House Press, 2016)

The Luminous Race Track: Memoirs in Poems (Lynx House Press, 2023)

Copyright ©2025 by Bill Tremblay

All rights reserved. No part of this book may be reproduced or utilized
in any form or by any means, electronic or mechanical, including photocopying,
recording, or by any information storage retrieval system without permission in
writing from the publisher.

ISBN: 978-1-935874-49-2

These poems are taken from the following books by Bill Tremblay:
Crying in the Cheap Seats (UMass Press, 1971)
Duhamel: Ideas of Order in Little Canada (BOA Editions, Ltd. 1986)
Rainstorm Over the Alphabet (Lynx House Press, 2001)
The Luminous Race Track: Memoirs in Poems (Lynx House Press, 2023)

Cover photo: St. Mary's Church, Southbridge, First Communion class, May 1948
Bill Tremblay is in the second row, fourth from the right.

This publication is funded in part by the *Southbridge Cultural Council*, a local agency
funded by Mass Cultural Council, and a gift from the *Southbridge Women's Club*.

Lost Valley Press
P. O. Box 122
Hardwick, MA 01037

lostvalleypress.com

Table of Contents

Introduction 1
My Town Is Called Southbridge 7
There Is Only One Endless Poem 8
Treetop High 9
Wardwell Court 10
The Advantage of Elm Street 12
In St. Mary's Church 13
After School 14
The Old Neighborhood 16
Creation 19
Unwritten Laws 20
Cabbage Night 22
Duhamel & Ledoux at the Bar, 20 Minutes to Closing 24
Redbrick Factory Blues 25
Central Street Breakdown 26
Tiny Tim As I Remember Him 28
My Uncle Pete 29
Nor'easter 30
Ecoute 31
High Requiem 33
Mother's Gladiolas 35
Jazz Memoir 36
Pushing My Bike Up Clemence Hill 38
Animation 39
After the Matinee 41
Gerry & The Sacrament of Music 43
My Father Drives Me to Amherst 45
Thanksgiving 47
Afterword 49
About the Poet 51

Introduction

My name is Bill Tremblay. I was born in Southbridge at 6:12 PM on June 9, 1940, at Harrington Memorial Hospital. The unusual circumstance of my birth is that the attending physician somehow forgot to make sure the obstetric nurse put silver nitrate in my eyes to prevent infection. The result was that my corneas were attacked by a virus which left them cratered like the moon—light was so refracted it could not reach my optic nerves. According to my mother's account, it took her six months of fearful denials to admit to herself that I was blind. She went to the doctor, and he did the right thing. He took responsibility and paid for an operation in a Worcester hospital where a surgeon made crescent cuts in my corneas and performed "tucks" which stretched the tissue well enough so that I had normal vision in my left eye. In my right eye—well, as they say, "not so much." My brain somehow managed to reconcile the quality of the two different images, but the result was never 20-20 vision.

When I was a boy in school it struck me as odd that I had this condition in a town known as "The Eye of the Commonwealth" in honor of the American Optical Company, which was the largest optical "plant" in the world. I wondered why a campus of eighteen brick buildings spread along the flood plain of the Quinebaug River was called a plant. Wasn't a plant a vegetable? That was the thing about me: I was fascinated with words, their meanings, their derivations. To call a building a "plant" was a metaphor, I learned. It signified the idea that a building designed for manufacturing was being compared to a living organism that transforms raw materials into a finished product.

I got my first pair of eyeglasses when I turned five. Three months later I entered St. Mary's Grammar School. Though my parents were both French-Canadian and spoke French, they decided to send me to St. Mary's instead of Notre Dame School because they later explained they thought it would be better to concentrate on English since we were living in the United States. I learned my alphabet. There was a square painted on the blackboard with numbers: one through twelve horizontally, one through twelve vertically, and all the multiples of all the numbers such that in the bottom right corner was the number 144. In the second grade my little classmates and neighbors (some of the kids from the Wardwell Court and Foster Street neighborhood also went to St. Mary's) were introduced to the Baltimore Catechism.

We were given the answer to "the meaning of life" way before we would ask the question in terms of any secular sense of childhood development. I still have a photograph of a large group of children (of which I am one) standing arrayed on the steps of the school, all of us dressed in white: the girls like little brides, some of them with veils, the boys in white shirts, ties, pants, all of us holding our hands in an attitude of prayer looking like a choir of angels. Human life was a drama, an adventure, a great going out from God and a return. We had been created in God's image like Adam and Eve and because they had committed the "original sin" God's only begotten Son had to die on the Cross (the pain was "excruciating," the kind of pain one could only get from being nailed to a large piece of wood) to "open the gates of Heaven," which meant that if we behaved ourselves according to the Ten Commandments and other regulations of the Church our applications for entry into Heaven would upon our deaths be carefully considered by St. Peter. It was infinitely more complicated than that (given mercy, love and forgiveness) but most of us were only seven or eight, having reached "the Age of Reason," as determined by the Sisters of St. Joseph and Fr. Smith, the parish priest.

Looking back, I have to say that the nuns gave me a good solid education, especially in the English language. They taught vocabulary through syllabics. English was made up of words from many languages: the one-syllable words came from Anglo-Saxon. The many-syllabled words came from Latin through French. Words with many syllables had a prefix, a root, and a suffix. You could learn many words from one root. For example, the root "press," from which you see "express," "repress," "depress" and by adding the suffix "expression," "repression," "depression," as in the Great Depression. All of our parents had suffered through it. In other words, there was a massive, almost incomprehensible structure to life, and a child with an imagination could wander in the realms of world history wondering what the evening air of ancient Egypt smelled like as Israelites baked their bread and set their tables for supper on the banks of the Nile.

We learned everything through Religion. For example, if the Bible said that "the sins of the fathers would be visited upon their sons even unto the seventh generation" and a generation was twenty years, then how many years would those sins need to be "expiated" (atoned for) until their curse was worn off? Simple: 140 years. That's how we learned arithmetic. We learned grammar by means of "diagramming sentences," by creating a kind of visual scaffolding using lines to graph the relationships between the main nouns and verbs and their modifiers, and dependent phrases and clauses that hang from independent phrases and clauses. There was in my mind also the wisp of an idea that sentences were living, organic things themselves. (I know that some of my classmates suspected that I was a weird kid, but I don't think they knew what was going on in my head and just how weird I really was.)

When I was thirteen I left St. Mary's and went to Mary E. Wells High School, primarily I think now to play football, which was the game I could play given my eyesight. I couldn't hit a baseball; I couldn't throw a basketball through a hoop. But I wanted to participate in sports, to enjoy that. So, as a lineman on defense or offense less than a foot away from another guy who absolutely did not wish to be moved, I didn't need good eyesight to move him, just strength and will. I could marshal my strength gained from carrying one-hundred pound sacks of grain at Weld & Beck's Feed & Grain Store on Foster Street starting when I was eleven. I could block and tackle and make it possible for the "skill" players to run and pass and score and win games with my help. I also read Shakespeare and learned Biology and Problems of Democracy and History and American, British, and World literatures. I memorized not only the football playbook but also my lines for school plays. I experienced the stunning arrival of rhythm 'n blues, rock 'n roll, and through my brother Gerry, West Coast jazz. And hot-rods, school dances at Notre Dame Hall, and everything else that the 1950s had to offer, "Rebel Without a Cause," Elvis, all at the Strand Theater.

So, in introducing this collection of poems about Southbridge I might say that they present my wonderings about the nature of life on this planet, human and otherwise (including not only the Quinebaug River but ghosts and angels and perhaps even demons) with Southbridge being the setting for all these imaginings. I wanted to know how things are connected. In effect, I wanted to know how God does it all, how He manages billions of thoughts, sensations, feelings, emotions, actions (often contradictory actions, actions that cancel other actions), things bubbling in scientific laboratories, wars, boys knocking frogs on the head with sticks, girls pretending to pour tea for their dolls, stars sparkling in night skies, crows squawking on powerlines, et cetera, et cetera, ad infinitum. Now, of course, I realize the enormity of the task of understanding, comprehending, it all. There have been bits of ideas I've picked up later in life. For example, I learned a story that helped me from the Gospel of St. Thomas. A disciple asks Jesus, "Heaven. You're always talking about the Kingdom of Heaven. But where is this Heaven?" And Jesus answers, "It is not something about which you can ask, 'Is it here, is it there.' Rather, it is all around us and we do not see it."

So a town is just a town or only a town, a collection of buildings with maybe paved streets and cars parked and people on sidewalks shopping on a Thursday evening. By analogy, a poem is just a poem, only a collection of words written or printed on paper, except that there's this notion of "reading between the lines," this notion that the words imply and that we as readers infer often something felt rather than known, a presence either of some sense of a spiritual being within things, within us, or a presence existing in things not commonly thought of as having spirit. Billions of years are contained within a stone. So the thing about these poems is that they are always implying something I feel but am tongue-tied trying to speak of, the mysteries that the nuns were always and forever pointing at as well.

Perhaps because of the kind of education I got in Southbridge, I see the town in mythic ways. It is Eden, Paradise, Heaven. It is a transcendent Southbridge, the setting where the drama, the adventure, the coming and going, the bright ideas and the terrible mistakes, take place. Each of us has a particular, a unique, way of seeing all this. These poems are expressions of my particular way of seeing and reflect my influences, which is why, maybe, I rely so often on the river since it is after all such a confluence of every spring, every hillside, every tributary and the whole thing has an origin and flows into the Atlantic which flows into every other ocean so that really there's only one ocean. Still, as I've gotten older I've been forced to face some limitations.

We humans are astonishing in our strengths and our weaknesses, our generosity and our selfishness. And there may be limits to what we can actually know scientifically, since with greater instruments we are learning that the universe is vaster and more mysterious than we have thought or tried to boil down to "the Big Bang." The point is that we continue to struggle with our limits, to wonder, to aspire, to reach, not out of greed but a genuine desire to find empathy with our world, each other, our universe.

Richard Hugo, one of my mentors, has this notion that every poet has a "triggering town," a place that could exist in memory or in imagination, that supplies them with the imagery and the cast of characters with which to concoct a world. The particular point for poets is that they should set the scene and as quickly as possible move from descriptive into figurative language—in other words move from informative or journalistic language into a language of the senses that carries a particular set of feelings that make the subject of the poem uniquely their own, a figurative language, a language of implication, a language charged with emotion. In effect, he taught me that I must find my own voice. The way he explained it was through an analogy with painting. "You know," he said, "when you go into a museum and there's a Picasso on the wall and you know instantly that it's a Picasso? That's what I mean about having your own style."

My style is mine but it is also every influence I've ever absorbed including the town of Southbridge. I think if there's one thing that moved me most is the sense I got of the working men and women of the town—how they sacrificed to give their children a good education and a future.

I believe I've received many gifts from the town of Southbridge, Massachusetts. And it's a town that's kept giving. I want to thank Margaret Morrissey, the wonderful director of the Jacob Edwards Library who has promoted it into the premier cultural institution in southern Worcester County, for helping Bill O'Connell, a former student at Colorado State University, and Jonathan Blake, Professor of English at Worcester State University, in their efforts to bring this book into the world. They were present on the occasion of my reading as the first Poet Laureate of Southbridge at the library when I mentioned my realization that poems about Southbridge are sprinkled throughout my life's work in poetry—enough to make a separate book of Southbridge poems. They approached Ms. Morrissey with the idea, and, voila! Here it is.

My town was primarily a factory town, a mill town, when I was growing up in it; it was a world into which I did not fit since my gifts were not mechanical, but verbal. Indeed, I had to go away searching for the right environment for my peculiar gifts to find a home where they could become the source of livelihood for me, my wife Cynthia, and my three sons—Bill, Ben, and Jack. But I've always said that Southbridge is a good place—especially in my case—to be from; the education I received whether parochial or public provided a solid foundation for advancement. Everything that any poet in any place and at any time ever had as a resource is also right here. The same challenges that exist elsewhere exist here—questions of how best to organize life so that with individual effort and faith in the future all of us can enjoy the amazing fact that we are alive and in a shared quest to become the best versions of ourselves we can.

This little book then is my version of "giving back." I hope that it will trigger good memories for those who remember the Southbridge that was and encouragement for those who dream of the Southbridge that will be.

— Bill Tremblay

From *Crying in the Cheap Seats*
UMass Press, 1971

My Town Is Called Southbridge

its streets and gutters
run with the rain
of my memory

every space in it
definite enough to be a place
has an episode of the endless poem
hidden like a demigod in it.

I make my Via Dolorosa
through the cobbling streets of this town
how it flowed into me
how the outside world like the Quinebaug River
flooded my town of ecstasy
away

There Is Only One   Endless   Poem

In the endless poem
there is a house   reared
in ecstasy   whose walls are
white screens where the ceaseless arc-lamp
projects through the sockets of my eyes
the energies between blood and galaxies

whose light reaches my chorded heart
strikes sparks from my bones
moves me, makes me   not   therefore I
but   sometimes always spread burning
along these three-tongued flames
intersection   and I am electrocuted.

I lay beside my brother   a while
he sleeps   I see
into the black rooms
a Canadian trapper,   a Norman
a mercenary Gaul for Rome   I am sick,
I know not why, I said to the dark lady:
It is guilt, she replied
you killed your own people for gold and salt.

And beyond him
a man waiting in a cave for dawn.

I was from the beginning
will and every shall be world
without end   Amen

Treetop High

at the powerline clearing
the hawk swayed
staring off east toward the cool ponds
when the flick of lead through leaves
sent him spinning into the sun

a pack of blue jays mobbed him
tearing at him with their beaks
until he circled back   exhausted

the hawk clutched the branches
with his talons, his eyes
sharp   his breast burning

and when he was hit
he spiraled down
and   still he was alive
screaming and fluttering in the laurel
until his head was bashed in with a gunbutt

and even when he was nailed
to the garage door
there was   still   that fire.

Wardwell Court

The court we live on is a dead end:
a cyclone fence
and then the light and power company

a hundred foot smokestack
coal burns   the sky is grey sometimes:
all night the transformers hum like locusts
to the sleepless

sitting on the steps I can see them all
the mothers   leaning out over railings
hanging clothes on spiderweb lines
from second-story porches   in housecoats

battling against the soot
screaming across the street "Chris d' Calvie!"
when one kid gets beaten up by another

they wash and cook
and love their husbands one night
throw them out the next, sometimes say
how they've been to confession to take
communion and no making love
hulking husbands stinking beer
and as if the Church were not enough
they go to a woman's house on Worcester Street
who drops two drops of olive oil   on water
and if they join it is the reason   the evil eye
a lot of them work the second shift
at the American Optical
I see them cutting down the sad path through
     the coal yard

and theirs is the death of cancerous mothers
and retarded children to be sent away to Belchertown

but mostly   it is   this picture
a mother shaking out a rug
on the back porch on a blue May morning
the month of Mary

she sings some simple song.

The Advantage of Elm Street

memories triple up
people dispose themselves in time

I leap Olympian from screen to screen
Southbridge poems jangle in my head
the catalog of merchandise on Elm Street

the fruits watermelon cantaloupe and cool
green seedless grapes in wooden boxes
in the street beside the cash 'n carry Colonnade
wagons in a row, bicycles   the mean kid and I
steal one, one Thursday shopping night
my momma   she pulled my pants down
and slapped my ass red for that one

I can hardly see straight
the Moroccan plunder of it all   the words.

Or in the Strand Theatre on Elm Street
all the world   Hollywood version   flickers
before me   Trader Horn in Africa   and
there were pretty tough chicks in butch cuts
and sat in the show with you on Saturdays

watching the impalas the cheetahs the giraffe's
fifteen-foot stride   I am the antelope
this lioness licks my loin
I can't stop looking at the superimpositions!

In St. Mary's Church

the ceiling is heaven
and lithe angels in flowing white robes
never quite smile.

On Friday afternoons in Lent
old   Italian ladies in black dresses
black shoes, balance on their knees
making the Stations of the Cross

genuflecting before the fiery pictures
their faces wrinkled with pain
like fingernails torn to blood
of the only Christ for them.

My endless poem began with that
every afternoon I go to pray that God
will grant me a wonder singing

but I have this vision: a high church
like a cliff   wind grey howling
from the mouth of a clouded sky
old people dumping the trash of their dreams
into that void it is God

I would walk outside everything astonishing
the ice on Hamilton Street
the houses the railroad tracks Quinebaug River
woods the high clay banks of Paige Hill
like the forehead of an Indian chief
the still early March sky above the stoic trees

everything sings its offering
oratorios penetrating the agnostic skies
my eyes could rise to the black above the sun.

After School

I spend my time
down by the Quinebaug River

down past the coalyards
the river runs hard
in lists between huge concrete blocks

they were going to erect
a trestle for the Grand Trunk Railroad
on those blocks

"They died on the Titanic, those people
that owned that railroad," my mother said.

I hear the steam-whistle over the North Atlantic
busted bulkheads   the iceberg horn
panic and song   the ark of lights goes dark under

and so they left these concrete things
unfinished, the paws of sphinxes.

These human associations
this residence in the earth
mix flesh with the wood and stone of
our habitations

the thin fingers of a sampan woman
I see her cooking beans on an open fire

moored along a Chinese river
she knows the endless motion   has worn it
thin on the stone mortar
grinding grain

    she knows the grinding motion
    of sex   the endless summer
    of the tropic
    just as the hawk knows the poem of flight
    his eyes blaze with a man pleasure
    his wings outstretched over a global updraft
    the lady wind swirling
    to make a hollow into the nest of the earth

the Quinebaug the North Atlantic the Yangtze
endless flowing, flowing through now.

From *Duhamel: Ideas of Order in Little Canada*
BOA Editions, Ltd. 1986

The Old Neighborhood

Yes, I go back there sometimes when I feel like
getting ripped. Maybe something I missed is
out in the open between the rows of three-deckers,
the tilted-over telephone poles with spikes
sticking out up to the crossbars, the constant
reminders. Maybe in the shadows under fifteen-
year-old sedans passed out in the gutter like
tugboats a ghost is jerking my chain.

This summer I saw that old d.p. we thought was
funny in his shirt with no collar shuffling
upstreet in the shimmering air above the hot tar
still talking to himself about his father's
farm in Macedonia. Over on the feed and grains store
loading dock, Brannigan was propping up a shoebox
with a stick on a string and sprinkling a few
teeth of corn as bait to snag a supper of squab.
His daughters're so mad at him crying God
cursed him with no son to carry on his name
none of them will cook for him anymore.

Duhamel's tenement is torn down, a few bricks
are left in the cellar hole. Three cement steps
leading up to nothing. They used to be third base.
The big elm was home. We'd be playing ball.
Duhamel would be painting out on the back porch.
I saw him paint a black stallion once with lightning
in his eyes. At 5:30 Marie-Paul would plod home
from the knife-shop after working hungover.

"Get a job," she gasped like Greta Garbo as she
plopped down on the ratty green sofa. "This is
my job," Duhamel answered, maybe wiping his hands
on a turpentine rag, maybe strangling it.

Homer Desjardins heard them if he was eating
supper outside with his radio. "They're at it
again," he chimed in that choirboy voice he
brought home from Normandy. "Some people just
can't take it," he chirped as he called the cops.
The cruiser tore down the street whirling up
dust like winter again with sand trucks spraying
in the same circular rhythms as mothers sprinkling
flour on pie dough. It was always the same charges
against Duhamel—drunk, disorderly, resisting

That cellar hole's like the one beneath all
the tenements you had to climb down into winter
nights to fill the oil tank that glugged three
times into the cold silence. You came to after
God-knows with numb feet for watching snow-
flakes fall through streetlight and remember
not everything that moves is living.

Duhamel would still be up painting, close to
his easel like they were ballroom dancers while
the neighborhood slept and snow covered the machines.
I saw him one night sway on top of his kitchen
table singing, "Humpty Dumpty had a great fall,"

as he splattered red paint on the floor. I guess
I'm not creative. All I thought of was how soon
six o'clock comes and walking to work in the dark

half-asleep with the wind biting your face, feeling
too old to quit and start over. We all wanted
something better. My grandmother often told me
she dreamed of the moon shining on the wind roaring
through the Quebec forests she'd never see again.
Why make yourself sad, I thought. We're here now
in this country. Duhamel never wanted to choose.
He'd stare into a blank canvas for hours
like it was the ocean where the ship that would
save him would show sail, him half-crazy with never
sleeping, with never letting the bonfire go out.

CREATION

In school the nuns taught God
made the heavens and earth in six
days. Duhamel never believed it.
He saw his mother and father make it
in one day.
                    At first it *was* dark.
His mother lifted the curtain and made
light shine through the glass windows
and the wooden crossbars, making their
children, the shadows.
                                His mother
carried him and created the kitchen,
the bathroom, talcum, pleasure. She
made the air, the smell of hot toast.
His father walked him with both hands
and created doors, the world outside,
angel clouds, and telephone wires strung
above streets where how things're connected.
He created motion in a maroon Packard,
and colors for go, stop, and maybe.

They created smokestacks, steeples, and silos
to mark the different kinds of work.
They created Revere Beach and, for
everything without end, the Atlantic,
with waves rushing toward him saying,
"Reverse. Everything in reverse."

Darkness came: light in reverse.
Shouting came: laughter in reverse.
Duhamel invented more uses for darkness,
the pleasures of making the world over.
Bathrobe sky. Melted tar night. Packard wind.
He hummed as his eyes opened in reverse.

Unwritten Laws

You couldn't climb into Bernadino's garden and
just take vegetables. He'd throw a brick at you
with his Mighty Joe Young chest muscles from
hauling lead in a wheelbarrow between surprised-
looking ripped out fire hydrants in the Water
Supply Company's back lot and the white-hot
crucilble, the plugs holding their twisted shapes
a minute before slipping like glacier walls into
a silver sea to be poured off again into molds.

When he came home after work to tend his tomatoes
neatly staked and tied with thin strips of white
cloth, he would know, or some enemy you didn't
know you had might tell on you because Jesus said
"The least to do to mine you do to me," and it went
both ways. Then you'd get it. You had to mind
the priests. If you had diabetes so bad the Boston
doctors said having another baby would kill you,
you still had to because God wants new souls.
But if Jesus died to save us all, why didn't history
stop? The priests said that was a mystery.

You couldn't walk on the Fong's front lawn
because Sarge slept under the porch in criss-
crossed shadows. His slobbery lower jaw sputtered
as he snored off his last bucket of beer. If you
shook his ground, his K-9 training would wake him.
Everyone knew Sarge could bite through chains and
put gouges in your thigh that turned purple then
yellow. You couldn't even think of paying old Lady
Gardino to poison his chow. He was a war hero.
He bit the butt of the Generalissimo. On Memorial
Days, Lyle Fong would leash him and march behind
Le Cercle Canadien Drum & Bugle Corps with a

doughboy helmet buckled to his head at a jaunty
angle with a cracked, dirt-brown leather chinstrap.
You couldn't play with yourself or you'd get like
Shakey Joe, spastic on the railroad track, and
what he did with his fly unbuttoned was awful red.
You couldn't swear within earshot of a dragonfly
or it would sew your lips up. That's why it's real
name was "flying needle." You had to mind the nuns
or they'd put you in the encyclopedia.

You couldn't go into the Central Avenue Spa.
Its show windows hadn't changed since the owners
went to New York City to celebrate Truman's miracle
come-from-behind victory over Dewey and saw stores
on 42nd Street with cheap telescopes lying tilted up
at fading stars warped on blue corrugated night sky—
its door the gateway to inside, whoosh of big electric
fan, a middle-aged man with a mustache waiting for
the counterman to stop serving two high school girls
cherry flips like he was asking them a big favor,
zipping panics at the window for cops who knew he'd
sell anything from behind the glass showcases with
their buck knives and Marine Band harmonicas.

A row of red plastic tuffets along the counter,
and beyond, two sets of booths where a rainbow mafia
jukebox gloomed the studs of leather jackets humped
over hamburgs from the grill black as a pagan altar,
floorboards showing through cratered tiles that
checkerboarded into darkness under the broken EXIT
sign and on out into God only knew what blind alley
where you would stagger some midnight because you
were only human in the hot beery stench of Dragon's
lost, bricked in, melting, begging for another
chance, looking up at a narrow strip of stars in
the shape of a big capital I.

Cabbage Night

Old lady Guardino jumped up from her rocker
at the thump on her porch. It was the night
before Halloween. The neighborhood kids whined
until their parents let them run loose in a pack.
They swarmed the garden fences. "Knick-knack,
break the witch's back," they chanted.

She was marked with the twisted right foot,
the sign of the goat, her high-laced boot pure
lead. She was the palsy in grandfather's hands,
the pink slip in father's pay envelope.

Into the rows they spilled, through dry
cornstalks like a starving drill-corps standing
at attention to a white, full moon. They tore
out the cabbages, running through the empty
hubbard-squash vines through the walkway
between the Fong house and old lady Guardino's.
They lofted the cabbages over her bannister
weaving like Apaches in a figure-eight crying
"Human heads! Human heads!"

She ran out, pouring a basin of scalding water
over the railing. Ghosts of steam sprang up
from wet angles—steps, the hood of a Ford parked
in the alley. "You're all in my power!" she cried.
"Go! Bring me more cabbage hearts. Fly!"
The kids stopped in their tracks.

Should they do as a witch had commanded?

First one child, then the whole gang
broke into a walk toward their three-deckers.
A chill crackled into the air,
shooing them along. Hot cider if they were lucky.
If they were lucky, no screeching dragon
clawing their hair as they tried to run,
feet stuck in sidewalks soft as fresh bread.
Old Lady Quardino stepped back out on her piazza,
gathering cabbages into her apron. "Good soup,"
she said to herself, the last words before dawn.

Duhamel & Ledoux at the Bar, 20 Minutes to Closing

"Fat chance I had," Ledoux sputtered, head
between his arms, a Pall Mall coiling white.
"I says, 'Is it some other guy? I figure
I'll work harder for her than anyone.
'I'm going to be the bride of Christ,' she says.
"My breath flew out of my mouth! How'm I gonna
compete with that? I can't change no water
into wine. I gotta pay like all the other suckers.
When she come back from the convent, I'd see her
walk down Hook Street near the California
Fruit Company loading dock, my chest'd start
thumping. Sister of Mercy, she was more
beautiful under the veil. She looked right
through me. From another world, I guess."
Ledoux stuck a shot glass into his right eye.
"She looked right through me," he said again.

Duhamel smiled. "Show her the knife in your back,
Ledoux," he said. "Show her the blisters in
your hands and feet. Be bold. When the Montreal
Express comes cutting through your rented room
like a huge refrigerator on wheels, say
'This world is blessed.' The kidney stone I pass
is a relic, a little razor. It gives visions.
A night in jail can make a blind man see.
The birds of morning can heat your coffee,
get you to work on time. The dead flies on
your window sill, though they perish, yet shall
they live to buzz again."

Redbrick Factory Blues

Hunched men with grave-shift eyes
wolfed fried potatoes and chops under spinning
blue-neon beer planets in all-night diners,
then dragged their bones to bed watching
moonlight carve angel cloud faces as leaves lifted
in unreachable pre-dawn treetop breezes.

Nothing so sticky as dog-day nights.
They let their war-weary minds float out
on jukebox waves in The Pink Pachyderm bar
as Patsy Cline stropped her love razor,
her voice reaching all the way downtown
to the Main Street jail
where grisly drunks snored on chain-hung bunks
and tenements where rhinoceros uncles
punched holes in plaster walls
through wallpaper layers covered with yellow
nicotine film of smoking families

as the men imagined her, brushing her hair
at a mirror singing about loving—not bad men
but those sick with gambling, whiskey,
whatever delirium they believed would lift them
out of fifty years of factory work,
dispel the nightmare of foreman ghouls
breaking their spirits, dancing on their graves.
I fall to pieces, she sang,
as bourbon violins pulsed in her veins.

Central Street Breakdown

Duhamel fell out of Dragon's Café
stumbling over filthy banks of plowed snow
north through alleyways to Hamilton Street
where in the display window of the furniture store
a round glass ball flickered like the witch's crystal
in *The Wizard of Oz*—
What was this thing, movies in your own home?
On this globe of black and white a big man
dancing in drag as Carmen Miranda with silly slapstick.
Struck dumb by the possibility that he was witnessing
the end of still pictures, paintings,
he imagined his forehead a camera
filming the slow blues of waiting taxies,
yellow in reflected office neon
where the town's only midget manned the two-way radio

Duhamel got a story going—A man and a woman,
peasants in olden-day China out to capture a white stallion
in a blizzard to win the patronage of their Lord,
the Provincial Governor of FuManchusetts.
Perhaps the wall of fog would choose their fate.
The Lord's trusted servants on a failed quest
cloaked in the white-out between Gregoire's Shoe Store
and the Unitarian Church—everything that wasn't China.

Duhamel buzzed as he caught the jazz-waltz
hi-hat of the Grand Trunk Railroad freight cars
clicking past the depot at 12:15 AM. Refrigerated cars
filled with dead Spanish-speaking revolutionaries, their lives
flashing out in silver glints and melted flakes on honed rails.
"Just like them Rosenbergs," Duhamel muttered,
mixing up decades in his sodden mind.
"Korea, Korea. Any small country
where red and white zombies kill to see
whose economy will rule the next century."
Duhamel groaned drunkenly into the feathery swirl.
Snow floated down past the lights of the Spectown Diner,
its one customer listening to Doris Day singing,
"Once I had a secret love" on the Mafia jukebox.
And away down the street an electric man
screamed his utter confusion in his glass world,
reading words in a mime's voice,
the empty gut of the poor sailing like yesterday's copy
of the *Southbridge Evening News.*

Tiny Tim As I Remember Him

Tiny Tim waddles on-stage,
the Harpo Marx of pre-war '60s
with angel ringlets and cheap ukulele
and big snozzola who paid no payola
singing lays of gentler days in terza rima,
karma do, his spindly legs are flying things
with pointy wings that barely bound
along the ground as he sang
dip dew drew da dewlips wit chew

when Ed Sullivan was god,
nothing changed, always the same goofy acts
rearranged, Chinese jugglers spinning
plates with sticks and talking dogs
delivering long comic monologs
as others took to the streets
wearing white sheets or sarongs with bongs
blowing smoke up Miss Vicki
while others died in Mississippi
to pay everyone's dues to Mr. Blues
as Bob Dylan, heir to Walt Whitman,
waited in the wings, tuning his strings.

My Uncle Pete

My mother gave him his nickname
English for *pauvre pitou* from when he fell
into a trash barrel fire and burned his ribs.

When I was a schoolboy I thought
he was like Icarus who flew too close
to the sun. He showed me his web of scars

like a beaten silver breastplate.
I wondered how much he could have
taught me with his Land camera,

the red glow of his darkroom,
the miracle of negative to positive.
I could've become a photographer

taking shots all over my home town
if I'd taken his suggestions to heart.
My first big coup would've been a thousand

suns reflected in a thousand factory windows,
then flecks of light on leaf tips by the river,
banks of candles flickering in St. Mary's.

I see myself being probed by reporters
for flip phrases during my first gallery show
unlike my Uncle Pete who lost the power of

speech from the shock of his burns.
I would have no struggle saying I don't believe
In the Sublime but the photos say different.

From *The Luminous Racetrack: Memoirs in Poems*
Lynx House Press, 2023

Nor'easter

Snow comes at us night and day,
sheets of snow, white cavalry charges
slashing the shingles off roofs.
Morning's the chill rigor of icicles
the size of scimitars.
We climb snowbanks to get to school.
Gusts make strings of light bulbs on huge
Main Street Christmas stockings jingle tinly.
The wind makes pagodas of triple-deckers,
roof angles smoothed into French curves.
Humps on Main Street are parked cars
that won't be shoveled out for days.
Hunched pigeons perched on clotheslines
watch neighborhood dogs romp and roll
in feathers from the sky.
Our mothers peer out windows,
prisoners of a glinting galaxy watching us
build snow castles. Oncoming dark
drifts over our crenellations flake by flake
into my grandfather Fontaine's ghost,
the one who called her Irene, the queen,
who made her something special.
We stomp our galoshes on the porch,
sweating hard beneath our woolen toques.
The kitchen smells of beef stew.
The setting sun's the wonder
we outlive the little Ice Age of 1948.

Ecoute

1.
A minuet echoes in Town Hall rafters
as schoolkids make bridges with arms
singing "blackbird, blackbird,
in and out my window,"
ducking, weaving with swept-back wings,
rehearsing for a talent show that night.
Some sounds soothe,
some shock like a hawk's shriek,
some rumble below human hearing,
a caterpillar inching cracks in sidewalks.
Some are fake like fat hairy wrestlers
grunting to make the whack
of cleavers hacking haunches
that don't really hurt at all.

2.
Vesper bells mingle with factory horns.
Men in Elmer Fudd hats, women in overcoats,
all in galoshes slush home, sleet stings
their faces, the *travail* of Adam's curse.
Aunt Lil says *Ecoutez et apprenez*.
I know the sound, like the waltzing rhythm.
She says jokes in French aren't funny
in English. Summers the ice-man
clomps up triple-decker staircases in his
orange rubber cape, tongs chunked in a block.

3.
Mme. LeBlanc in flowered house dress
opens the door with a *Comment ça va, George?*
Vegetable men charge down Wardwell Court
in a pick-up, singing their obbligato:
Tomatoes, potatoes, cu-cumbers,
ripe juicy melons straight from the vine,
sound patterns, the four-act saga of snow, rain,
wind, ice, as clouds roll back
curtains of factory smoke.
Dizzy's father's drunk again, slips on salt sand.
His wife married a child
and now must put him to bed.
Fish men appear from stinging ocean swells
with tuna from the Outer Banks.
On their radio a woman sings,
See the pyramids along the Nile . . .

Car brakes screech, a dog whimpers.
People on Central St hold their breath.
Silence, the birth of sound. Sound, the death of silence.
And in that death the womb of more sound.
My mother and father speak French to keep their secrets.
I agree. I don't want to know.
A woman sings *Allez vous-en, allez vous-en*
on my mother's Victrola.
English is my mother tongue, the life-raft I cling to.
If Paradise is our true home,
u'est-ce c'est, mon petit, qu'est-ce c'est?

High Requiem

We float on a white fog of incense,
a rising to and falling from
fires that neither light nor burn.
A hundred Hail Marys will shorten
time served in Purgatory.
What sin could my *grand-mère*.
she of graham-cracker Sunday
crayon coloring books be punished for?
Through isinglass church floors
her face appears as rusted lilies.
How can a bodiless soul suffer pain?
A spirit's agony is loss of union with God.

A stained-glass dove hovers above
the altar with a green sprig in its beak
selected from the Michael-angelic palette.
Nine spheres of angels
form the gravity of Heaven
we feel as the crown of conscience.
Archangels don't fly. They just appear
to announce the calcium age
in human bones on sidewalks.

No matter our digressions
in the glassy red asylums of dusk,
everyone takes the shock of cold air
we're born into. I press each bead so hard
my thumb bleeds. No one escapes
the sins they're blessed with.
Hell is below Purgatory, Limbo's above,

Earth is God's battlefield with the sly Seducer.
And the sodality of sinners
comforts all but the innocent.

Walking home along its west bank
the Quinebaug narrows to a sand-spit
I see an orphan trash barrel
with flames licking soup can labels,
a smashed baby crib. My prayers reach out
to those who lived and loved
before Jesus kicked open the gates of Hell
and whipped the demons
who would not release Socrates
without a fight,
the unremembered sinners in my blood,
my undocumented family who kneeled
before the thrones of lust and greed.
I deposit my rosary in God's bank
hoping it will open the transepts of His mercy
now and at the hour of our Gethsemane.

Mother's Gladiolas

After Easter, on a warm day,
past when daffodils rise from snow
she unwraps the bulbs she keeps in burlap
all winter. My job is
to turn the soil with a trowel,
sprinkle in compost. She places each
bulb a hand-length apart.

Purple petals with yellow wattles
appear by mid-May.
They sway on breezes in the alleyway
between triple-deckers where factory workers
pass to punch the clock.
I can touch the soft blooms
if I'm careful not to bruise them.

From Memorial Day to Labor Day
no one picks or tramples them.
A janitor in overalls takes a knee
to smell their muted fragrance.

Some internal clock turns them
rusted brown in late August.
My job is to dig up the bulbs
and wrap them in wet burlap.
She celebrates the green parts of the year.
I think she makes the seasons change.

Jazz Memoir

I play Fats Domino on my portable.
Gerry says to listen to the sax section.
It goes *ta-da-ta-da-dah-dah*.
He says he can teach me to play that
in ten minutes. He puts on "Somewhere
Over the Rainbow." Donald Byrd and Gigi Gryce
jump an octave on the first two notes.
A door opens in my chest. Everything is technicolor.
Gerry Mulligan and Chet Baker
trade off on "Tea for Two."
Never heard a bari sax before,
baugh-be-baugh, be-baugh, be-baugh.
I spend a winter at Fontana's Record Store
on Elm Street next to the Strand Theatre.
Chico Hamilton, Art Pepper playing
heartbreak San Pedro fog.
Mrs. Fontana never expects a high school kid
to dig West Coast jazz. If liking jazz means
I'm weird, Amen. Charlie Parker sounds
like an egret burbling
on the back of a yawning hippo.
Mrs. Fontana says she can't deal with so much
beauty in the spectacle of a junky genius
who turns tragedy to threnody through a reed.
I long to be on the side of beauty without the junk,
but will pay the price the Boatman asks.
I walk like Demosthenes in solo lamentations
where bleak dawns
become the first flutings of larks.

Pushing My Bike Up Clemence Hill

It goes in stages: first Paige Hill
my legs like pistons through sludge,
my body arched like the Central Street bridge
over the Quinebaug, grinding up past
St. George cemetery where afternoons vanish
cracking pig nuts under wild
grape vines draped over tree limbs,
listening to the speech of birds.
Clemence Hill is another stage my legs are
never in good enough shape to conquer.
I push the blue Columbia bike
my uncle Bill gave me for my birthday
with a kringing bell, spritelier than the grave bongs
of Norte Dame's bell tower. With a bike I can
go anywhere and be back for supper.

Near the crest, I stop to admire
six milk cows lying carefree
in a pasture of lemon yellow dandelions.
A silver milk truck grinds uphill
to McKinstry's farm. My forehead cools,
the sky grows dark as birches
peppered with crows tilting their beaks,
making love-croaks as they squawk,
rehearsing for a Saturday cartoon show
where they chomp ears of corn
then snap their craws back
with a ding like typewriters.

Hail pops on tarmac, the sound of Gene Kelley
singin', dancin' in the rain, *ka-lick, ka-lack,
ka-lickety klick, ka-lock, splash, splash, splash, splash!*
The one beam of light breaking through is
Debbie Reynolds' smile, the flash of her legs
as she spins her pleated skirt and falls on the sofa.
I lie down in green pastures wondering
where is the girl God wants me to love?

Animation

1.
I learn in school the Latin word *anima* means soul,
a film of breath on a mirror or a spark of life God gives.
Sr. Monica comes out to the ballfield.
Her cowl arches like the Hollywood Bowl.
I'm on my toes at third, ready for a hot grounder.
I tell her I'm going to see *Pinocchio*. She forbids it.
The talking cricket she says is a pagan demon,
a false conscience. I've seen the previews, I'm going.
Nights are so hollow since my brothers and sister left.
I hear my mother turning in her bed at night.

2.
Theater lights dim. Curtains part.
A still picture of a clear starry night, then stars
begin to sparkle. Animation. My heart begins to beat.
The cricket sings in so mellow a tenor
it could never be false.
I really do believe wishes can come true.
Geppetto has put his longing for a son in every tap of his chisel.
Out of the stars a blue Lady descends in a bubble
like an immaculate conception.
She gives the puppet speech, but he isn't a real boy yet.
His smile is only painted on.

3.
Next morning his father sends him off to school.
Honest John sings *Hey diddle-dee-dee* . . .
It's easy to lure him to the puppet circus. He's never met a liar.
Pinocchio sings and the audience throws gold.

You've had your fun, now you must pay!
thunders Stromboli, the human volcano.
He locks Pinocchio in a cage without supper.
Again, the Blue Lady sails down from the sky and frees him
only to learn Geppetto went looking for him
and got swallowed by a whale called Monstro.
The wooden boy sets out to save the family
that set out to save him.
How he changes happens inside me.
A frozen river melts and starts to flow.

4.
I walk from dark theater to dark streets.
It must've rained while I was away.
One step for magic, one step for miracle.
Perhaps Sr. Monica's bad review is a quibble
over who owns the franchise.
A wish and a prayer. *Quelle différence?*
A puppet who learns to think of others becomes a real boy.
My eyes are twin projectors. I see my brothers and sister
in the blurred reflection of a puddle.
They sleep in my dreams where I keep them safe.
I'm not anymore the baby of the family.
To tell a story that quickens the heart is a miracle.
Some words are images with a living soul inside,
a cricket with big human eyes
who listens for a whistle.

After the Matinee

Sundown spreads its golden syrup
through the elms of an August evening
as my father smokes
a Pall Mall and sighs thinking of his
father dead alone in Worcester's skid row
"from exposure," he says. "To what?" I ask
in the always-present. He crushes his stub.
"Can Billy come out?" Kenny asks
through the screen window. Everyone's there:
Stashu, Dizzy, Bernie, the two Carols.
"Can I?" "You and your gang going to terrorize
the neighborhood?" he teases.

The screen door slaps behind me
as I jump off the porch. We walk up the alley
between tenements singing "Around her neck,
she wore a yellow ribbon. She wore it in the winter
And the merry month of May. When I asked her
Why the yellow ribbon she said it's for my lover
who is far far away. FAR AWAY, far away,
she said it's for my lover who is far, far away . . ."
singing as if we knew what wearing a ribbon
as a token of someone we love
feels like as we float into the elm grove
our baseball diamond,
up the outfield where Stashu will always
shoot an arrow in my shoulder
and the scar will always mark that moment
as we go past old lady Guardino's
and we sing past the Fong house and circle
the neighborhood like a cavalry patrol.

That's what keeps me going
when things go south: kids singing as the stars
come out. And mothers echoing our cadence
calling us home on account of darkness.
Is there one place I can go
that always lifts my heart?
Yes.

Gerry & The Sacrament of Music

Thursday night, shopping night,
Gerry drifts on a sinuous cloud of
hot buttered popcorn
wafting from the Five & Dime.
He's a teen-aged shambling gawker
maundering up Main Street,
a lover of crowds and sidewalk bazaars.

Like a cartoon cat lifted off his feet
by a can of tuna opening,
a ribbon of sound draws him
upstairs to *Le Cercle Canadien* Hall.
A drum and bugle corps rehearses a Sousa march.
The band leader hears him in the stairwell
humming "Stars & Stripes Forever"
and hands him a horn.

The guys in the corps take five
as he puts the mouthpiece to his lips.
His cheeks bulge like Gabriel
and out comes one clear note,
a home run on his first at bat.
The way Saul becomes Paul
on the road to Tarsus, Gerry is changed.
He plays *O happy day* over and over
until sunlight spills from him
and the earth becomes
the only planet of music in the Milky Way.

His mission now is to find
the right tone for every note,
to run the scales like a robin on stick feet,
to spiral in a brass communion
with his friends on the diamond-studded
staircase of Dixie as they play
"South Rampart St. Parade"
shuffling on the neat little rhythm
of happy dancing feet.

When I look at the sheet music
all I see is dots like crows on a rail fence.
When I tell him how happy I am for him
he looks at me over the bell of his horn.
I have notes, he says. You have words.
When you get the urge,
ask yourself if what you write
has a heart. Does it know
how changed chords make changed feelings?
He finds all that in his horn,
a threshold to the universe within,
a "Glory, hallelujah" ready to begin.

My Father Drives Me to Amherst

He knows the poet recited verse
at Kennedy's inauguration,
but only asks how much he got paid.
Or was it, like every time
a working stiff gets screwed, *pour l'honneur?*
This from a man who dreams of
getting rich betting on horses.
I try to explain what this poet's job is:
to quarrel with God,
to praise the dead and put them
in poems with their families
whether the families want them or not.
You think you can live on what you imagine?
he asks as he masters the winding road
between West Brookfield and Ware.
I sit beside him like a one-legged sparrow
as we drive through budding spring woods.

At last we enter campus.
I slip into the back row and listen.
The poet brushes off his critics like snow
fallen on his shoulder.
A death wish, he chuckles.
He doesn't count the decades of ice,
the bitten prayers, the sudden blood
of saw-blades run amuck, blizzards of crumpled paper
filling his waste-basket, candles snuffed at dawn,
Another day's dawn so dazzling his red eyes sing.
He recites a poem about a brook
with boulders that fling white waters

back to their source.
It's the closest he gets to God.
For my father it's when he hits the Daily Double.
I don't wonder about him.
I wonder what the poet means
by bringing sleeves of ice into the iambic sway
of girls with their hair thrown forward
in the shattering of a crystal January.

I see my father with new eyes
standing outside the Student Union
smoking a Pall Mall,
reading horses' names in *The Racing Form*
in a slant of evening light.
He looks studious in his tweed jacket
and gabardine shirt like an old scholar
at a university park in Quebec City.

Thanksgiving

Thanks for the aluminum pot
my parents gave me when they hopped a bus
for San Diego. Thanks be also for
the potato masher with its diamond holes
the mush squirts through
as I mix in butter and whip it to Arctic peaks.
Praise be the annual flooding of the kitchen
with roast turkey aromas of pork-pie stuffing,
all that's left of my family's Canadian past.
Is it true that origins are destiny?

Ma yells: *Raymond Jay Tremblay!*
Sonny winks: *Oh-oh. What'd I do now?*
I give thanks for his smile that tells me
not to be afraid of Ma's voice
that sounds the Last Judgment.
Why does she call Sonny Raymond?
She bastes the turkey with a bulbous eye-dropper,
hands me the masher. *Your father and I we
baptized Sonny Raymond. After we married
he got a job as a milk-man in Somerville.*
Somerville is a movie set
where an actor spins a yarn in a spotlight
with soap flakes for falling snow.
She takes in laundry. The baby is Nancy.
Her brother is born bow-legged.
His Ma makes his shins grow straight
with her magic hands.

Soon he roams Beacon Street
looking for the action.

One time he doesn't come home.
They look everywhere, down brick alleys
where winos pass a bottle. It gets dark.
They find him watching a dance marathon
with couples hanging on each other
like everybody else in 1933.
Dad's pay envelope is so thin
there'll be no turkey that Thanksgiving.
They give him their last thin dime
to buy a church raffle ticket.
He comes home with a turkey bigger than he is.

Maybe his nickname gives him
a sunny disposition. It's hard to be humble
when your name is Raymond, king of the world.
Maybe we'll never know
the weight a first-born carries,
blazing a trail through the deep dark forest.
I give thanks for my brothers and sister.
It turns out better than any of us expected.
I give thanks to the river that taught me
abundance and gave me
poverty in spirit and richness of heart.
I give thanks to Dee Sharp as I dance
the mash potato and use a wooden spoon
to sculpt them into a replica of Plymouth Rock.

Afterword

I went to the writing program at Colorado State University in 1982 for 2 reasons: a teaching assistantship and the mountains. I didn't know about Bill Tremblay. I remember the day he brought this large boulder covered with moss and dirt into the poetry workshop and plopped it on the table: WRITE! he commanded, and we did. In *Form & Technique*, Bill used chalk like a conductor. He taught us as much about poetry with his hands and facial gestures as with what he had to say. Which was plenty.

In his imagination and in his poetry, Bill returned to Southbridge again and again. For any writer, the place of growing up is a force that stays with you. Think Kerouac's Lowell or Martins Ferry for James Wright. Something about a company town past its prime holds so much power in the worker-citizen relationship: when it goes, the whole town goes with it. The power of machinery and those who run it: when it stops, when the wage worker is left on the curb.

Tremblay's father was a truck driver. His mother raised a family and worked at the largest employer in town, American Optical. It is their lives and their neighbors' lives as well as the local kids running in and out of doors that make up the cast in these Southbridge poems. And behind it all is the poet re-imagining, seeing this townscape and what was left to ruin. In the poem *My Town is Called Southbridge* Tremblay writes: *its streets and gutters/run with the rain/of my memory* and later: *how the outside world like the Quinebaug River/flooded my town of ecstasy/away*. Indeed, Southbridge is a "Triggering Town" for Tremblay: the flow of the river and the flow of voices on Wardwell Court where the young poet watched and listened:

> sitting on the steps I can see them all
> the mothers   leaning out over railings
> hanging clothes on spiderweb lines
> from second-story porches   in housecoats
>
> battling against the soot
> screaming across the street

Tremblay writes in ***Duhamel***: "Yes, I go back there sometimes when I feel like/getting ripped." It's not Bill himself but an avatar descending again and again upon Southbridge to retrieve what the past holds, what it gives up.

Bill Tremblay is in many ways a jazz poet. In the least, jazz and improvisation are infused into his work. He credits his older brother, Gerry, for bringing home jazz. Richard Simpson in a review of ***Duhamel*** wrote: "Tremblay's language resembles the articulate but torrential *sheets of sound* for which John Coltrane became famous." Here Bill re-imagines through Duhamel his own discovery of jazz in the smokey apartment rooms of 1950's Southbridge:

> Duhamel watching Frances talk hot and drowned out by
> the 45 EP playing on the Webcor with its fat,
> brown spindle of Donald Byrd and Gigi Gryce
> turning "Over the Rainbow" into a bop pole vault
> through the gates of Oz.
> *(Duhamel Brings Home a Young Hobo)*

It was Gerry who set for Bill the lifelong love of jazz music and those propulsive solos in his poems

Tremblay's work is often on a search, whether for the truth about Trotsky's death in Mexico in ***Shooting Script,*** or for French Canadian myth in his beloved Poudre Canyon beyond Fort Collins where his novel *The June Rise* is set, or his own wanderings in the foothills of the Rockies feeling the land and history underneath his feet. But Southbridge is the beginning and end of this search, the fulcrum around which the poet pulls. For what? His French-Catholic identity? The sources of his art? Unlike Duhamel, Tremblay the artist left town. But it never left him, and he didn't let it. He knows the power of place.

— Bill O'Connell
Author of *Sakonnet Point* and *When We Were All Still Alive*

BILL TREMBLAY is an award-winning poet, novelist, teacher, editor, and reviewer whose work has appeared in ten full-length volumes of poetry including *Crying in the Cheap Seats* [University of Massachusetts Press], *The Anarchist Heart* [New Rivers Press], *Duhamel: Ideas of Order in Little Canada* [BOA Editions Ltd.], *Shooting Script: Door of Fire* [Eastern Washington University Press]. Hundreds of his poems have appeared in literary magazines  and in such anthologies as the *Pushcart Prize, The Jazz Poetry Anthology, Best American Poetry, 2003*. In 1994 he published his novel, *The June Rise* [Utah State University Press], which was widely and favorably reviewed, especially on NPR's "All Things Considered." In 2004, his book, *Shooting Script: Door of Fire* received the Colorado Book Award. He has received awards and fellowships from the National Endowment for the Arts, the National Endowment for the Humanities, as well as at Yaddo. He was a Fulbright visiting Lecturer at Universidade de Lisboa, Portugal. Mr. Tremblay edited *Colorado Review* for 15 years and is the recipient of the John F. Stern Distinguished Professor award for his thirty-three years teaching in and directing the MFA in Creative Writing Program at Colorado State University. His latest book is *The Luminous Race Track,* [2023], poetic memoirs about growing up in his Franco-American working-class family in the town of Southbridge, Massachusetts where he has just been appointed the inaugural Poet Laureate. He is at work on a new collection of poems tentatively entitled *Signs & Wonders*.

www.ingramcontent.com/pod-product-compliance
Lightning Source LLC
Chambersburg PA
CBHW032100040426
42449CB00007B/1150